MW00744388

From:

mom 2 mom

7 Reasons to be Grateful You're the Mother of a

blended family

Kathy Vick

New Leaf Press

A Division of New Leaf Publishing Group

7 Reasons to be Grateful You're the Mother of a Blended Family

First Printing: December 2006

ISBN-13: 978-0-89221-654-3
ISBN-10: 0-89221-654-9
Library of Congress Catalog Number: 2006937329

Cover and Interior Design: LeftCoast Design, Portland, OR 97219
Printed in Italy

For information regarding author interviews, please contact the publicity department at (870) 438-5288.

Please visit our website for other great titles:
www.newleafpress.net

table of contents

To Pippi and her ugly sister.
You rocked my world and
stole my heart.

Kathy

CHAPTER 1

Gratefulness

means we get a

do-over day

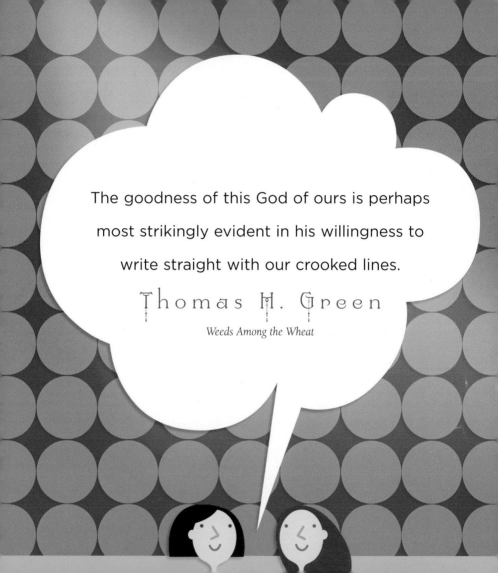

I'm so sorry—You did not deserve to be yelled at."

Andrea and Patrick just looked at me like they hadn't

really noticed that I had just displayed a complete lack

of control. Without looking up they responded, "It's okay,

Kathy, we forgive you." They seemed completely unscathed

and rather surprised I would even bother with a confession.

Their reaction was a stark comparison to how I forgive

myself. As a mother, the bar has always been set high and if I fall, I must not be trying hard enough. My reality is that occasionally I lose it, blow it and with that comes the predictable self-loathing for not having it all together. It's an ugly place, where I stand guilty, in need of forgiveness.

It reminds of the story in John 8 about the Pharisees dragging the woman caught in adultery before Jesus. He utters those jaw-dropping words, "Let he who is without sin cast the first stone." Can't you hear the stones falling from weary, stubborn hands? Can't you feel the relief of the woman standing guilty, yet forgiven?

The twist to this kind of "do-over" is being open enough to receive the gift.

God says a rock is a rock is a rock. Let it go.

To hear those rocks tumble to the ground even when we know we deserve it. It excludes no one. So the mom who worries she is not there enough, present enough, or simply enough, gets the gift, too. God says a rock is a rock is a rock. Let it go.

One day my next-door neighbor asked me if I had heard

her yelling at her kids. I replied, "No," secretly wondering if this was her gracious way of telling me to keep it down. Instead, I discovered that she was confessing to me.

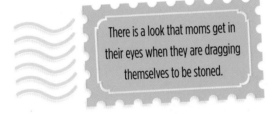

There is a look that moms get in their eyes when they are dragging themselves to be stoned.

There is a look that moms get in their eyes when they are dragging themselves to be stoned. She had that look. I put my hand on her shoulder and reminded her that we do not have to beat ourselves for the moments when we fall from grace. There is another way, a do-over promise from God. Weight lifted from her face and tears replaced her words.

The stone tumbled down.

One of the most difficult scriptures to walk is "Do not judge lest you be judged yourself." It speaks to the practice of "do-overs" that begins with a single choice to live in the presence of forgiveness, to not run from grace but be steeped in its fragrance. This is the gift that draws the line in the sand and asks us to choose life over death—an allowance for a mother's imperfections. There is no other way but to let the rock fall.

Gratefulness

says a sense of humor is

the best medicine

My laugh is like a sonic boom. Proverbs refers to this mixture of raucous joy as *good medicine*, something I came to count on when I married a man with two children.

Presto! Wham! Swoosh! I was an instant wife and mom. It was like stepping into shoes that didn't really fit, but shoving my foot in all the same. This kind of life change makes the sane woman crazy, stressed out, and just a little lost. With all the best intentions I tried to fix things, compete, make peace, and generally save everyone around me. Those shoes were killing me.

When she blurted it out, it suddenly became clear I was a rookie and this whole motherhood thing was going to take some time.

I remember getting a call from my 11-year-old daughter. "Uhm, Kathy, I'm in the vice principal's office, because I called a boy a jerk." Not having any experience with these kind of situations I immediately sprang into defense mode and told her I would be right there.

Upon arriving at the school, I had my whole speech rehearsed. Especially the part about how calling someone a jerk, while not the best choice, was not profanity. So I got there and gave my little speech and the vice principal just looked at me and said, "Mrs. Vick, I think Andrea has something to share with you." I turned my eyes on my daughter who had lost all color in her face and she said, "I didn't call the boy a jerk, I called him a bad name." When she blurted it out, it suddenly became clear I was a rookie and this whole motherhood thing was going to take some time.

Laughter creates space for grace.

During my initiation into this new role, I would meet my friend Karen for laughter and coffee—in that order. I can't put into words the value of being in the company of another woman who "got it" and could help me step away and laugh. It was like a transfusion that made me *want to* survive another day.

Laughter, after all, is God's ammunition for the crises, comparison, and conflict that come with motherhood. Did I mention the dramas? Today, I got a frantic call from my daughter, who was late for a job interview. I dropped everything and got her

there with a minute to spare. Still holding onto the door in the seat next to me, my neighbor Kay said, "Wow, I never knew you could drive like that." We both laughed at what seemed to be an everyday event—moms performing superhuman deeds.

Laughter creates space for grace. My husband and I have both struggled during our kids' launching years. We've wrestled with a 22-year-old whose goals do not include college but would walk across glass to get to a Sci-Fi convention, and an 18-year-old who thinks she is 30. One day I told my son that sometimes his dad and I lie in bed at night and giggle, imagining him dressed as a Star Wars-Jedi. His reply: "Yeah, but imagine me in a really *well-designed* Jedi costume."

Laughter is therapy on call. So if my not-so-dainty laughter makes me look crazy, I really don't care. If my Jedi knight fuels my funny bone, it's good medicine. Laughter is like having *diamonds on the soles of my shoes*. So, like the Paul Simon song goes, *"they help me lose my walking blues."*

CHAPTER 3

Gratefulness

means we are thankful that

God has a plan

We owe twenty thousand dollars to the IRS." After speaking those words, my husband scanned my face trying to anticipate my reaction. I left my body and sort of hovered over the room in shock. I remembered thinking I had never owed that kind of money before in my life. I kept asking, "Are you sure? How could this have happened?"

I wish I could tell you that we spent it on a fabulous vacation to the Italian Riviera, which is decidedly more interesting than using it to pay for attorney's fees, private detectives, and child psychologists. For those of you who have prepared for court, you know that the cost is daunting. When you are in the middle of it it's hard to predict how it will all shake out .

"Shake out" is a good description of what happens to our lives when we're faced

> Sometimes he is silent, at others like a tour director...

with challenges we have never had to meet before. To God, this is fertile ground when we come to him scared, confused and faithless, asking to see the plan. Sometimes he is silent,

and, at others, like a tour director, is revealing a design so
exquisite in its mathematical perfection we call it "impossible."

Two weeks later I was sitting in a church service and my eyes
rested on an announcement for a job opening for a publications

director. The next month I started my new position. In less than a year we were able to pay our entire debt to the IRS.

> As I listen to him he sounds less like my 22 year-old Rock Star and more like the boy I've seen in the 8mm movies . . .

God's big plans are often not as much about resolving the immediate need as a complex set of events that lead us to something we had never even considered. A year later, I went to spend some time with a designer who I had met while working in my position at the church. That visit resulted in a five-year consulting job with the design firm he worked for ... culminating with the production of this book. I have to consider if we hadn't owed money to the IRS whether I would have gotten here.

So when my son calls me at 12:30 in the morning because he has a notice on the door of his apartment making vague threats of eviction, I feel his pain. As I listen to him he sounds less like my 22-year-old Rock Star and more like the boy I've seen in the 8mm movies of his childhood. Standing in my robe in the dark, I know with complete confidence there is a plan of mathematical perfection. Smiling, I assure him something truly magnificent has already been designed.

Gratefulness

means we are thankful

for the people in our lives

No story sits by itself. Sometimes stories meet at corners and sometimes they cover one another completely, like stones beneath a river.

Mitch Albom

The Five People You Meet in Heaven

People are like translucent layers that touch our own. Sometimes when they leave, small pieces stick to us and become part of who we are. Sometimes they stay and become our people.

"They" stuck to me right away. Patrick and Andrea knew intimate details of my life, from how much coffee I drank to what I looked like at thirteen at the peak of acne and general geekiness. They are born comedians who can imitate my laugh, my gestures and remember every stupid thing I've ever said or done in the last eight years. They are Kathy Vick experts and sometime fans.

They are survivors with trusting natures...

Through the years, my kids have fought with me, cried with me, and resented me. Most importantly, they have given me courageous, persistent love. They are survivors with trusting natures who graciously took me for the "real deal." They have never wavered in their belief in me and even when we are arguing about smoking cigarettes or religion, the glue between our stories is solid. They are my people.

My grandma Gladys used to stand with her hands on her hips on the front porch of her South Dakota home. "Kathy," she would say, "remember you are a Boice." Meaning, "Don't do anything to embarrass our people." While extinguishing any thoughts of mischief, this also planted the idea that people

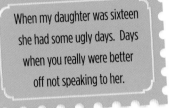

When my daughter was sixteen she had some ugly days. Days when you really were better off not speaking to her.

claimed me as their own. I was a part of something solid and secure. It came at a particularly poignant time in my life because I was in those years between finding something of myself and being lost.

When my daughter was sixteen she had some ugly days. Days when you really were better off not speaking to her. An innocent glance would result in her head spinning around, demanding, "Why are you looking at me that way?" For her birthday I had put together a scrapbook of every picture I could lay my hands on and I wrote her a poem. The title was

"Claiming Andrea". Sometimes, I told her, it is when we are at our most ugly that we need to be reminded that we have people. There may be nothing more important.

Eight years ago, my family claimed me. Their stories lie beneath mine, hard won. We could have given up on "us" many times, because building a family has many ugly days. The miracle is that we stayed.

"I claim you in the midst of it

In the ugly, messy grip of it...

You are mine and that's the end of it"

Written for Andrea, 2004

CHAPTER 5

Gratefulness

means we thank God

for the job

N egotiating debit cards and driving rights with
teenagers is like training starving hyenas to jump
through flaming hoops. You don't know whether to
feed them or light yourself on fire. My parents sat quietly
by, observing this parley of parent and potential adult. Later
my mom told me, "Dad and I were marveling how all the

experiences in your life prepared you for this job."

"What? You're kidding, right?" I thought. Then I stopped and tried to wrap my head around the idea. What could have possibly prepared me for this? I had often asked God why he had put me in this invisible, unrecognized, and overwhelming position. His answer: "I chose you."

Where do you go with that? Choosing me for a job that

rubs against my gigantic need to be recognized and appreciated?
Knowing that I always went the extra mile for any position I
held? Knowing my grave imposter insecurities? Knowing I
would never give up?

As jobs go,
motherhood is by
far the riskiest.
What lies behind
the greeting card

What lies behind the greeting
card sentiment is messy, hard,
scary, painful, selfless work.

sentiment is messy, hard, scary, painful, selfless work. This is the
kind of work you are only willing to do when you share blood
and bone with someone and can remember their every sweet
baby moment.

I don't have those memories to bank from. My kids call me "Kathy," not "mom" and

> I appreciate every mom who recognized that I was operating from an impossible place and extended me grace.

I have no on-the-job training. Honestly, being thankful for this job wasn't my first thought. More like, *Who do I register my complaints to?*

So when I think about what there is to be thankful for, I find that I am thankful for *blender moms* like you. Moms who may not get the title, but whom God prepares and sends to perform risky, uncomfortable tasks out of line with what we thought we could do.

I appreciate every mom who recognized that I was operating from an impossible place and extended me grace. I stand in awe of every blender mom, who falls in love with her kids regardless of blood and bone and who gives from bottomless reserves of love.

> Like me, you may never be able to be thankful for the "work" of this job.

Like me, you may never be able to be thankful for the "work" of this job.

Bottom line, no doubt your life has prepared you for this risky adventure, and in the end it won't be about why God chose you, but about *who* you become in the process.

CHAPTER 6

Gratefulness

means we thank God

for our strengths

and weaknesses

The first time that my daughter tried to do an end run around me, I was traumatized. Andrea squarely placed herself between her father and I, resulting in an argument. It was ugly and I felt my anger and a deep sense of betrayal burn in my heart. I tried to reason with my darker self. *Step away; let it go* was my mantra. It felt like another woman (albeit a teeny-weenie-woman) had come between me and my husband. My weaknesses, jealousy, pride, and "the controller" inside me all refused to shut up. What resulted was a wound for all of us.

I hadn't really considered Andrea's needs, because my own had spilled out with rage. I hadn't considered other options or opportunities; instead, I fell into the very trap laid for me and, by the time I realized what had happened, the damage was already done.

I fell into the very trap laid for me . . .

Those of us who have step-daughters understand that there is great probability, that at some point in time, this

loving admirer to whom you have given your best makeup—
and how-to-get-out-of-a-car-in-a-skirt tips will turn on you. At
least that is how it feels. The truth is that, gone unchecked or
resolved, this kind of division can bring down relationships
and marriages.

It can also be an opportunity to get real—to speak honestly about our fears, our weaknesses. It's a chance to tip the scales in a new direction. A chance for God to show His strength in our weakness. To see us through honest, loving eyes.

Sometimes I am the heroine, and sometimes I am her broken counterpart.

It's a drama that it is continually at play in my life, strength best revealed through weakness. The constant tipping of the cup. Sometimes I am the heroine, and sometimes I am her broken counterpart. Amazingly, God loves both.

I have had many weak, unbeautiful moments as a mom. They run together like a blur of time and create a place of knowledge within

myself that I am still imperfect, prideful, and lost. I contain other things as well . . . strong, beautiful, loving things that God planted deep within, long ago. It is God's eyes that help me be honest about the tipping cup, to see and even embrace my own humanity.

CHAPTER 7

Gratefulness

means we thank God

for the journey

We left the paved road just outside West Glacier

to travel on gravel for fourteen miles to the tiny

town of Polebridge, Montana. Pat and I looked

at each other with a mix of excitement and apprehension.

Fourteen miles seem like forty when you only pass one truck,

with driver, gun rack, and four dogs. While we negotiated

potholes and wild life, the thought crossed our minds that we might be lost. As the gravel road turned into a muddy path and back to gravel, we couldn't imagine that we would find anything worthwhile at the end of it.

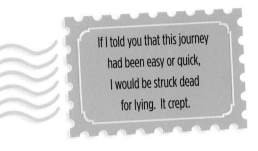

If I told you that this journey had been easy or quick, I would be struck dead for lying. It crept.

The road changed like that the day our two kids moved in with us. Pat and I had many plans that were waylaid that day and if I told you that this journey had been easy or quick, I would be struck dead for lying. It crept. Much like the ride to Polebridge, Montana.

No doubt the Israelites felt many of these things on their

way out of Egypt, through the Red Sea into the desert. "Great," they must have thought. "This is exactly what I had pictured."

Blending families may not take forty years—it just feels that way. Family is made while we are trying to negotiate the potholes, the wildlife and the ever-changing road. From tense visitations, non-existent child support and the challenges of keeping our kids' feelings first even when we wanted to drive a stake in the heart of their other parent. Most days we were traveling gravel road.

I remember Christmas visitation plans that fell through at the last moment. There we were, realizing that our romantic weekend for two was not going to happen. Instead, we decided

to take the kids along with us to the romantic B&B in Vancouver BC, where the hostess broke her rule of "no children" and our kids put on their best manners.

Christmas day dinner was eighty dollars a plate and seven courses. We laugh at the memory of Andrea asking the very proper waiter for more tater tots only to be told they

were "croquettes." Later, she emerged from the restroom with
the back of her dress tucked in her tights. All this and a trip
to Chinatown, where an eel got loose in a fish market and
both kids tried to help everyone grab it and club it over the
head. It wasn't what any of us had planned for Christmas,
but we were grateful for the change in the road.

The thing is, all journeys are like this,
and the destination of a life may be best
summed up by the promise of lots and lots
of gravel roads and few smooth ones.

When we finally arrived at Polebridge to have dinner
at the Northern Lights Saloon, we delighted in finding a

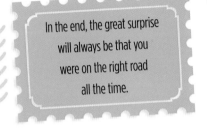

In the end, the great surprise will always be that you were on the right road all the time.

wonderful place not many tourists will go, because the road doesn't come easy and there is always the possibility you might take a wrong turn in the woods.

The thing is, all journeys are like this, and the destination of a life may be best summed up by the promise of lots and lots of gravel roads and few smooth ones. At times you may not see that anything worthwhile will come of it. In the end, the great surprise will always be that you were on the right road all the time.

We're thankful you've chosen to explore

7 Reasons to be Grateful You're the Mother of a Blended Family.

f these essays have made you recall your own for-better-or-worse moments, take a few minutes to write some thoughts to perhaps share with your child(ren) sometime... like after they have their *own* kids.

How Many Do-Over Days Can We Have?

Sometimes during a long string of seemingly wasted days, we long for meaning, purpose, and some guarantee this child-rearing gig will turn out positively. Is there a time you can look back on, now from a different perspective, when the dreariness of day-to-day family duties produced a bit of hope after a long, dry spell?

Immediately following 9/11, New York Mayor Rudy Giuliani suggested we needed to find a way to laugh again—while we're still crying. Some might suggest this applies to motherhood as well. Can you recall some times when laughter gave way to tears . . . and tears gave way to laughter?

What's the Master Plan?

It's been said that life has to be lived forward, but can only be understood backward. As a mom, what experiences have you had that have shifted your view of your plans versus God's plans? In what areas are you still hoping your plans will win?

As Hillary Clinton noted, it takes a village to raise a child. Who are the members of your tribe, your people? How have they helped you raise your family? In what areas do you feel you *have* to go it alone?

Some say parenting is the only job for which we apply without a clue of what we're doing. Do you view parenting as a chore? A job? A gift? How has it been different from what you expected or hoped for?

D o you feel hand-picked by God to parent your specific kids? Does this notion change your view of your own strengths and weaknesses?